Reims Travel Guide, France

Information Tourism

Author
Leon Shaw.

Publisher:
SONITTEC LTD
College House, 2nd
Floor
17 King Edwards
Road,
Ruislip
London
HA4 7AE

Table of Content

Summary

Why Travel and Tourism Is More Important Now Than Ever

I believe that travel expands our minds, broadens our perspectives, and teaches us tolerance to cultures and mentalities that are different from our own. More importantly, travel opens our hearts and makes us more humane and compassionate towards others.

When we travel especially across borders we see that people are fundamentally the same, despite differences in culture, religion or belief. No matter what happens between countries and governments, people are people. We are all searching for the same things: a better life, a better future for their children and more purpose.

Finding Positivity and Hope

Amidst all the negativity surrounding the world these days, we need to find more positivity and hope in our lives. And travel lets you do just that. Travel spreads love and shows us the goodness in people.

I've lost count of the number of encounters I've had with people who have touched my heart. Because of this, the importance of travel to me has always been incredibly clear.

Like that time when I lost my wallet in Tirana, Albania and a young man helped me out by lending me some money and making sure I got home safely.

Or the other time when I couldn't find my way out of the maze-like old town of Yadz in Iran, and a middle-aged man kindly gave me a free lift and even invited me to have tea with his wife in their home. And another time when I fell sick while biking around Bagan, Myanmar, and a kind lady who was selling drinks on the streets ushered me straight into her stall and nursed me for hours.

Albania, Iran and Myanmar are all places that many consider "dangerous", and yet the people I met there are some of the kindest souls. What we read on the news are just that the news while individual stories are what we really need to hear, and yet they remain untold.

I cannot stress how different the stories on the ground can be to what we see on TV or in the newspapers. I recently traveled to Brussels and Istanbul just a few months after the terrorist attacks. And as I expected, everything actually had returned to normal, besides the few additional security measures. Once again, it goes to show that reality is different from what the media feeds us. So get out there and see for yourself. The world really isn't such a scary place.

The importance of travel is still great
In times of distress like these, we need travel. We need more love and positivity in this world.

We need to unite and stay together, because we are always more powerful as a unit. There's a need for us to choose good over evil. We need to believe in others and see the beauty in people and the world once again.

If we stop traveling, we stop flourishing. We stop accepting people who are different to us and we stop connecting with the world. Let's break down borders and build bridges that connect all of us because together, we can fight fear by traveling.

Introduction

Reims, also spelled Rheims, city, Marne département, Grand Est région, northeastern France. It lies east-northeast of Paris. On the Vesle River, a tributary of the Aisne, and the Marne–Aisne canal, the city is situated in vine-growing country in which champagne wine is produced. It is overlooked from the southwest by the Montagne de Reims.

The Gallic tribe of the Remi (from which Reims derives its name) was conquered without difficulty by the Romans, and the town flourished under their occupation. In the 5th century, Clovis, the Frankish king, was baptized at Reims by Bishop Remigius (Rémi), and in memory of this occasion most French kings were subsequently consecrated there. (Charles VII, for example, was crowned there in 1429 in the presence of Joan of Arc.) The traditional wool industry was stimulated in the 17th century by King Louis XIV's finance minister, Jean-Baptiste Colbert, who was a native of Reims. During World War I, the city was occupied briefly by the Germans in their offensive of September 1914, and after evacuating it they held the surrounding heights, from which they subjected the city to intermittent bombardment during the next four years. In World War II Reims was again almost completely destroyed, although the cathedral escaped damage. The act of Germany's capitulation in World War II was signed at Reims in May 1945.

The 13th-century cathedral of Notre-Dame, greatly damaged during World War I but admirably restored, ranks as one of the most beautiful Gothic churches in France. Although its building took more than a century, it has a remarkable unity of style. It has a harmonious facade with graceful and expressive statues; fine 13th-century stained-glass windows (restored); and a collection of reliquaries. The basilica and abbey of Saint-Rémi, begun in the 11th century, was also damaged in World War I, but its interior, with a narrow nave, an early Gothic choir, and 12th-century windows, is still striking. An imposing 3rd-century triumphal arch is one of the city's few remains dating from Roman times. The cathedral of Notre-Dame and the abbey were collectively designated a UNESCO World Heritage site in 1991.

Reims is an administrative and commercial centre. Together with Épernay, it forms the industrial centre of the champagne wine district. The wine is stored in large cellars tunneled in the chalk that underlies the district. The nature of the soft stone, however, has led to collapse of some surface structures into the caves, endangering the city's architectural heritage. Engineering, chemical, and packaging industries are also important. The city is home to the University of Reims, Champagne-Ardenne, and a large conference centre. An airport lies about 4 miles (7 km) north of the city centre. Pop. (1999) 187,206; (2014 est.) 183,042.

About Reims

Reims in Champagne Ardenne is renowned as the city of the coronations where the French kings were crowned in the impressive Reims Cathedral.

Founded by the Gauls as Durocorteron, which became a major city of the Roman Empire, Reims has a vibrant history that has taken in some of the most important events of the 20th century as well as being the site of the French coronations. Monarchs stayed at the beautiful Palace of Tau before their coronation and the Sainte Ampoule was brought from the Abbey of St Remi to the cathedral in order to peform the rites of anointing. All three buildings, as well as the

Basilica of St Remi, are recognised UNESCO World Heritage sites today and are all unmissable visits whilst in Reims.

A visit to the area is not complete without sampling some of the region's most famous product - champagne. With several champagne houses in the city and vineyards all around, you are spoilt for choice to find your favourite champagne. Reims is however, well known for less happy reasons, as over 80% of the city was destroyed during WW1 and the ruined cathedral, which has since been restored, became one of the most important images for anti-German propaganda in France. In WW2, General Eisenhower and the Allies in Reims received Germany's unconditional surrender that ended the war. Following the destruction of the city, much of the city centre was rebuilt during the 1920s in the Art Deco style with some stunning geometrical patterns on the buildings and arcades.

With such a long and interesting history to explore, it is hardly surprising that Reims has several great museums. The St Remi museum inside the abbey of St Remi houses four collections related to the city - the history of the abbey and its tapestries, a Gallo-Roman archaeological collection, weapons from ancient times to 1870 and a history of the city from prehistory to the 16th century.

The Fine Arts Museum is housed inside a part of the former Abbey of St Denis whilst the former Jesuit college contains the collection of the Regional Fund for Contemporary Art (FRAC) of Champagne Ardenne and has a planetarium outside. The world wars reserve special attention with the Museum of the Surrender at General

Eisenhower's War Room containing the Signing Room where the act of unconditional surrender was signed and Fort de la Pompelle Museum which holds collections of uniforms, weaponry, artillery and a unique Friese collection of 560 items of headgear that belonged to the German Imperial Army.

There are many sites of rememberance across the city with war memorials to the nurses, martyrs of the Resistance and to the dead of Reims as well as the soldiers who died in the war. More museums and sites of rememberance including cemeteries and locations of battle can be found in the area around Reims. Other sites worth visiting include the Château de Condé, the Gallo-Roman cryptoporticus, and the Place Royale dedicated to Louis XV. The city has some great parks and gardens with the 12 hectare Parc Léo Lagrange and the historic Parc de la Patted'Oie created in the middle of the 18th century. Why not go for a hike in the nearby Parc Natural Regional de la Montagne de Reims or take a trip in a hot air balloon to explore more of the countryside that this beautiful region has to offer?

Visit the champagne houses of Reims to enjoy some champagne and understand the process of making this world renowned wine. Producers including Mumm, Champagne Pommery and Champagne Lanson all have champagne houses in the city and champagne Lanson gives tours of its vineyards, the production process and its wine cellars. Reims has many specialist food and wine shops where you are sure to pick up a bottle of local bubbly, perfect to enjoy with some chocolates from Reims' great chocolateries.

The Espace d'Erlon is an excellent shopping centre in the city centre for all your needs - fashion, health and beauty, jewellery, multimedia and more and there is at least one market in the city every day. Whilst in Reims don't forget to try some of its famous biscuits rose (often enjoyed dipped in champagne) and gingerbread which has a unique taste due to the use of rye flour instead of wheat flour. Dishes made with champagne are popular including poached pears in champagne and fillet mignon au champagne (veal in a champagne sauce). If drinking champagne all holiday seems too extravagant then why not give the new Reims drink Café de Reims a try? A coffee made with Montagne de Reims whisky, whipped cream and crumbled biscuit rose, it is the new speciality of the city.

History of The Reims Cathedral in France

Once upon a time there stood the Reims Cathedral in a kingdom not too far away. This beautiful lady towered over the city, showing off her beauty and acting as the center point for all who wanted to meet and gather to worship (or just gossip as many were prone to do before the telephone, emails and text messaging). It took 100 years for her to grow to her full height. Kings were crowned within her walls, babies baptized and sermons preached.

And then the war came.

SIGNIFICANCE OF THE REIMS CATHEDRAL

The cathedral of Notre-Dame de Reims, France was built over a 100 year period in the 13th century. Another one hundred years added the French kings to the façade, reminding the public that at least 25 French kings were crowned within the walls of Reims Cathedral. Why Reims? Clovis, the king of the Franks, was baptized here by Bishop St. Remy around 498 A.D., making it sacred ground for royals, especially since French kings claimed their rule was ordained by God. Legend tells us that St. Remy received a vile of oil from a white dove. This holy oil crowned every king up until Charles X in 1825.

Reims Cathedral saw many changes in the world, but none so devastating to itself than World War I. This cathedral was repeatedly shelled for over four years during the war. Eighty percent of the city of Reims disappeared between 1914 and 1918, as Germany relentlessly attacked France and tried to bring the country to her knees. The front line was just outside of Reims, and the cathedral was the largest target. Residents tried to protect the cathedral, placing sand bags at the base, which did help to protect the lower statues, but many of the magnificent features were lost. More than 300 shells fell on the cathedral during the war, melting away the iron roof and wooden interior.

Residents come back and began to rebuild in the 1920s. Arguments arose as to whether the cathedral should be rebuilt or if the ruins should serve as a reminder to what was lost, plus there was no money to rebuild. The Rockefeller Foundation donated money to resurrect the cathedral, so reconstruction began. Many of the surviving church statues were placed in the Palace de Tau museum with copies replacing the originals in Reims Cathedral.

Some of the celebrated stain glass windows from the Notre-Dame de Reims were spared by a family of glass makers who removed the windows they could and meticulously took others apart piece by piece so they could hide them and protect them from the shelling of WWI. These 12th generation glass makers then helped to restore the original glass into the newly rebuilt cathedral and replaced windows that were destroyed beyond repair with replicas.

One of the only surviving windows, the North Rose Window from the 13th century, sits above the church organ and depicts twelves scenes of Adam and Eve, and the fall of man from God's grace. This "Window of Creation" miraculous made it through the shelling of WWI, while its sister window, the South Rose Window, which depicts the beauty of Christianity, exploded during WWI. It has since been recreated, but is a mere copy of the original.

While World War I caused the most devastation to the city, Reims was again hit during World War II, but the Reims Cathedral stood proud over her city, taking on much less damage than she did in the first World War. On May 7, 1945 the allies signed the treaty to end WWII in Reims in the school room where General Eisenhower had set up his headquarters.

Reims Cathedral has seen princes, kings, queens, babies, and soldiers walk through her doors, sometimes proudly showing off her beauty, while other times praying for war to end. The walls continue to speak of what has happened throughout the city of Reims, the changes that have occurred in the city and society as a whole. Now she waits to see what will happen in the next one hundred years as man continues to evolve, and hopefully learn from the mistakes of the past that once brought the Reims Cathedral to her knees.

Quirky Facts About Reims and Reims Cathedral

The statues at the top of Reims Cathedral weigh about four tons and stand four meters high. Many of the Reims Cathedral lower statues heads are missing. During the French Revolution, revolutionaries chopped the heads off, which was later put into practice with real people via the guillotine. The church and crown were directly linked, which is why revolutionaries took out their frustrations on the statues.

The icon of Reims is the smiling angel, which stands just outside of one of the main Notre-Dame de Reims doors. Her head fell down during WWI. There was a great celebration when her head was finally reattached as it symbolized to the city that they were finally recovering from WWI.

Before WWI the streets of Reims were narrow and hard to navigate, as the city had grown over the centuries, expanding for more family members, shrinking when disease or war hit, and growing again as modern life took over. After WWI, John Ford from New York was commissioned to draw up a new city plan, which included wider streets, gardens and a more organized layout. Citizens were encouraged to rebuild and were given the freedom to pick which style they wanted their homes built in. You will easily find more modern, art deco structors next to gothic-style homes, making this city a fascinating hodge podge of architecture and style.

Reims Cathedral Light Show

Every May through September (and then again for the holidays) the city of Reims hosts a spectacular light show at the Notre-Dame de Reims cathedral. This is no ordinary light show though. It is a work of art. This UNESCO World Heritage site is one of Europe's most important gothic structures. The city recreates what they think Reims Cathedral looked like after it was first built. Church facades were created to teach the local residents Bible stories, as many of them could not read at the time, and also the history of their country. The light show at Reims Cathedral, lasting about 20 minutes, depicts how historians think the cathedral looked when it was painted and the stories they might have told

Tourism

With a Gothic cathedral that dates back more than 800 years, venerable Champagne *caves*, playful Art Deco style, and vibrant pedestrian zone, Reims is intoxicating. And thanks to France's slick high-speed train network, it's just 45 minutes from Paris making it an easy day trip.

Reims (pronounced like "rance") has a turbulent history: This is where French kings were crowned, where Champagne first bubbled, where WWI devastation met miraculous reconstruction, and where the Germans officially surrendered in 1945, bringing World War II to a close in Europe. The town's sights give you an informative, entertaining peek at the entire story.

Start at Reims Cathedral a glorious example of Gothic architecture and one of Europe's greatest churches. Built under the direction of four different architects, the church was started in about 1211 and mostly finished just 60 years later. Thanks to this quick turnaround, it's remarkable for its unity and harmony. As a royal coronation site, it is to France what Westminster Abbey is to England.

For a memorable experience, join the crowd in front of the cathedral for a free, 25-minute sound-and-light show on most summer evenings. I've struggled with the idea that some of Europe's wonderful Gothic church facades were boldly painted in the 13th and 14th centuries. In Reims, the sound-and-light show did a good job of helping me envision how they might have looked to a medieval peasant. Sit directly in front of the cathedral or settle more comfortably into a seat at a café with a clear view past the trees.

When wonderstruck by Gothic cathedrals, I often contemplate the lives of the people who built these huge buildings back in the 13th century. Construction on a scale like this required a community effort: It was all hands on deck. Most townsfolk who participated donated their money or their labor knowing that they would likely never see it completed such was their pride, faith, and dedication. Master masons supervised, while the average Jean-Claude did much of the sweaty work. Labor was something that even the poorest medieval peasant could donate generously.

In addition to spiritual nourishment, Reims offers a more earthly delight Champagne. Though many wine-growing regions in France produce sparkling wines, only the bubbly beverage from this region can be called Champagne. While the ancient Romans planted the first grapes here, Champagne was not "invented" until the late 17th century, and then it was by virtue of necessity the local climate and soil did not produce competitive still wines.

According to the story, in about 1700, after much fiddling with double fermentation, it was in nearby Hautvillers that Dom Pérignon stumbled onto the bubbly treat. On that happy day, he ran through the abbey, shouting, "Brothers, come quickly...I'm drinking stars!" Today the result is commonly regarded as the finest sparkling wine in the world.

Reims offers many opportunities to visit its world-famous Champagne cellars. All charge entry fees, most have a several daily English tours, and most require a reservation (only Taittinger allows drop-in visits). Which should you visit? Martel offers the most personal and best-value tour. Taittinger and Mumm have the most impressive cellars (Mumm is also close to the city center, and offers one of the best *cave* tours). Veuve Clicquot is popular with Americans and fills up weeks in advance. (Cazanoveis closest to the train station and the cheapest, but you get what you pay for.) Wherever you go, bring a sweater, even in summer, as the *caves* are cool and clammy.

If you find yourself strolling across town to a Champagne cellar, keep an eye open for *biscuits roses*light, rose-colored egg-and-sugar cookies that have been made here since 1756. They're the locals' favorite munchie to accompany a glass of Champagne you're supposed to dunk them, but I like them dry (many places that sell these treats offer free samples).

Allies surely celebrated with Champagne on May 7, 1945, after Germans signed the document of surrender for all German forces. WWII buffs enjoy visiting the Museum of the Surrender (Musée de la Reddition), the place where it happened. The news was announced the next day, turning May 8 into Victory in Europe (V-E) Day. The museum has an extensive collection of artifacts, but the most thrilling sight is the war room, where Eisenhower managed Allied operations and where the European part of the war ultimately ended.

Though World War II left the city unscathed, World War I had devastated Reims. It was the biggest city on France's Western Front, and it was hammered around 65 percent of Reims was destroyed by shelling. Parts of the city center were entirely rebuilt in the 1920s. That's why the town is now dotted with the stylized features geometric reliefs, motifs in ironwork, rounded corners, and simple concrete elegance of Art Deco. If it looks eclectic, that's because the mayor at the time said to build any way you like just build.

With all this history packed into a vibrant cityscape, Reims feels both historic and youthful at the same time. Each visit here reminds me of how much fun it is to enjoy modern French culture in a sizeable city that isn't Paris.

City of Coronations and Champagne, Reims can be proud of possessing four historic buildings that are inscribed on the UNESCO World Heritage

List: the Notre-Dame cathedral, the Tau palace, the Saint-Remi basilica, and the Saint-Remi museum.

The jewel of the city, the Notre-Dame cathedral is unusual in that it has been the place of coronation for 33 kings of France from 816 to 1825. Clovis was also baptized in this place in 498. The architectural harmony and remarkable statuary of this 13th-century building make it a masterpiece of Gothic art. Decorated with magnificent statues of angels with opened wings, the cathedral of Reims is really worth its nickname of Cathedral of Angels. Once inside, one is immediately attracted by the brightness of the nave and the magnificent stained glass windows, which date largely from the 13th century. Don't miss seeing the blue stained glass windows of the axial chapel, designed by the contemporary artist Marc Chagall.

Next to the cathedral, the Tau palace, a former archbishop's palace where the coronation banquets were notably organised, is today home to the Works of Notre-Dame museum, where tapestries, sculptures, the cathedral treasury and coronation-related objects are exhibited.

The next of the Champagne city's historic places to visit is Saint-Remi basilica, a magnificent Romano-Gothic building, and its museum. Situated in the buildings of the former Saint-Remi abbey, the museum recounts the history of the abbey and houses art collections from Prehistory to the Middle Ages.

Also not to be missed in the city: Place Royale square, surrounded by arcades, and Place Drouet-d'Erlon square with its lively cafés, shops and restaurants.

The museum-mansion Le Vergeur, installed in a mansion of the 13th and 16th centuries, is home to art objets, furniture and paintings.

Famous for its buildings, the City of Art and History of Reims is also well known for the cellars of its prestigious champagne houses, which are dug into chalk and open to visitors.

Additional Information

City of coronations, City of champagne... Reims is eager to unveil the legacy of its glorious history and immerse yourself in the prestigious world's most famous and most festive of wines.

Rich traditions and know-how secular, Reims has also become a regional metropolis modern and dynamic thanks to its location at the crossroads of several trans-European routes, its highly diversified economy and its teaching excellence and research.

Four sites on the List of UNESCO World Heritage, the refined atmosphere of Champagne Houses, a city immersed in an atmosphere imbued with both the elegance of Art Deco facades and streets and relaxed the lively cafe terraces, an abundant and varied program of events, a natural environment where green is king... Reims opens its doors and welcomes you.

A two thousand year history...

Ancient Reims: Legend Reims was created by Remus, brother of the founder of ancient Rome. The Celtic people who inhabited the region have thus taken the name of Remi. Around 80 BC, they established an oppidum they named Durocortero ("round fortress"). After the Roman conquest, Durocortorum is integrated into the province of Belgium and became the capital. At its peak, with its 30 000 inhabitants, the Gallo-Roman city became one of the most populated north of the Alps.

Around 260 is founded the bishopric of Reims. During the great invasions in 407, Bishop Nicaise is massacred by the Vandals in front of the church he had built. He became the patron of the city of Reims.

The baptism of Clovis: The baptism of Clovis, King of the Franks, by Remi, bishop of Reims took place on Christmas Day 498 in a baptistery whose site is now occupied by Notre Dame. The conversion of Clovis to Christianity, religion of a church heir of Roman power, allowed him to legitimize its military grip on Gaul then divided.

It was after this baptism, which sealed the reconciliation of Church and State, born as the monarchy of divine right French. It's also thanks to him that Reims become the seat of the coronation of the kings of France.

The city of coronations: In 816 occurred the first royal coronation in Reims, that of Louis the Pious. The ceremony, usually five hours long, took place in the Cathedral of Notre Dame, since it was built. She continued by the coronation banquet at the Palais du Tau and a pilgrimage to the body of Bishop Remi, in the basilica dedicated to him. The most memorable coronation remains that the dolphin Charles VII, led to Reims by Joan of Arc July 17, 1429 after the siege of Orleans. A total of 33 sovereigns have been crowned at Reims, the latest being Charles X in 1825.

In the Middle Ages Reims prospered by selling her sheets, linens and other textile fairs in the south of Champagne and trading with the

Hanseatic League. The rise of champagne, from the reign of Louis XIV, came complete range of its productions.

Two of the most famous sons of the city, Jean-Baptiste Colbert, Comptroller General of the King's finances, and Jean-Baptiste de La Salle, precursor of modern pedagogy, Reims were born in the seventeenth century.

Modern Reims: As elsewhere, the industrial revolution overthrew the appearance of the city, who spent 30 000 to 120 000 in less than a century. Rich mansions replaced the houses with wood sides. Some of the first international airshows were held in Reims early twentieth century. Reims is indeed one of the cradles of aviation.

Then came the First World War. On 4 September 1914, a month after the beginning of hostilities, the German army entered Reims. It was quickly rejected, but she dug in the forts around. Hence, the Wehrmacht bombard the city for 3 ½ years. The cathedral, very hard hit, will receive nearly 300 shells. The seat will result in the destruction of 80% of the city and killed more than 5,000 victims.

The new Reims, which rises from the rubble in the interwar period thanks to the intervention of 325 architectural firms, has a face full of eclectic in its architecture, marked in particular by the Art Deco style.

The Second World War affected the little town. During the conflict, welcomed Reims the headquarters of Eisenhower. This is where, on 7 May 1945 at 2:41, General Alfred Jodl, supreme commander of the Wehrmacht, signed the unconditional surrender of Nazi Germany. The text, drafted in haste by members of the staff of Eisenhower, was to put an immediate end to the conflict. It was ratified in Berlin the following day by the heads of allied states.

On 7 July 1962, the German Chancellor Adenauer and General de Gaulle sealed at Notre Dame reconciliation between the German and French peoples and Reims erected as a symbol of peace between Germany and France.

Quick Guide to Reims

Reims, the home of Champagne (the most celebrated and celebratory wine in the world), is the main city of the Champagne area. There stands one of the most beautiful buildings of the Middle Ages in Europe, one that is filled with history: almost all French kings were crowned there for about 1,000 years. Most of the old houses were destroyed during World War I, and the city was extensively rebuilt in the 1920's in an Art Deco style.

Reims, Épernay and Ay are the main places of champagne production. Many of the largest champagne producing houses, referred to as *les grandes marques*, have their head office in Reims. Most are open for champagne tasting and tours by appointment only. Champagne is aged in the many chalk caves and tunnels, some originating in the Roman period, located deep inside the ground.

The city centre is fairly small and easily walkable, with many streets for pedestrians only, mainly in the shopping area.

To Get in

Since the high speed train line has been opened, Reims is linked not only to Paris, but also to major cities in the country: Lille, Bordeaux,

Nantes, Strasbourg, ... Charles De Gaulle airport is only 30 minutes away and offers good connections to the South-East (Lyon, Avignon, Marseille, Nice, Montpellier). Trains to cities other than Paris leave from the brand new Champagne-Ardenne TGV station, located just outside the city. This station is connected to the central station through bus and local train. When booking your ticket, check the station you'll be arriving to or leaving from as many people get mixed up and miss their train

Although one can get cheaper tickets if travelling on the regular train lines (with a change of trains in Épernay), it will take over 2 hours and one might get a much better deal buying a TGV ticket a few weeks in advance.

To Get around

While the centre is fairly compact and easy to get around by foot, if you want to go further afield then try the buses. They're very reliable, run regularly and despite local complaints, I think, a good value at €1 to go anywhere. If you intend to use them a lot, buy a carnet of 10 tickets for €8.60 from bars, tobacco shops or newspaper stands. Single tickets can be bought on the bus but make sure you have the correct change. You can also buy day tickets for €3 which is worthwhile if you take the bus at least 4 times during the day.

There are two tram lines in the city. They share a similar route but the B line goes to the new Champagne-Ardennes TGV station. Trams on this line can be very infrequent. If you're looking to catch a train at Champagne-Ardennes, it's best to book from Reims Central instead of relying on the tram.

Trams use a smart card ticketing system. Note that you must 'touch on' to the readers on the tram, even with the paper tickets.

Taxis are reasonable (about €2 a mile) but you can't hail them and they have to be booked in advance, which can be difficult if your French isn't above conversational level.

With the TGV a day trip to/from Paris is possible (it only takes 45 minutes). Be aware you have to book in advance, but at least you can do this in English online at www.voyages-sncf.com.

To See

Cathedral (Notre-Dame de Reims) - the French equivalent, somewhat, for England's Westminster Abbey, the cathedral at Reims was the church in which numerous French monarchs were officially crowned. Reims is one of the later Gothic cathedrals and renowned for its height.

There is a fine interior west facade with carvings of Biblical scenes; some fine 13c stained glass in the high windows of the nave and choir; and windows by Marc Chagall (in the eastern chapel) and the two local artists Jacques and Brigitte Simon. The south transept window by Jacques Simon shows themes linked with champagne including a portrait of the monk who invented it, Dom Perignon.

- ✓ The Palace of Tau was the archbishop's palace and retains a 13c Palatine chapel.

- ✓ The Porte de Mars - a large late-Roman period triumphal arch

- ✓ The Hotel de la Salle - a fine Renaissance mansion

- ✓ The so-called Hotel des Contes de Champagne is a fine Gothic merchant's house.

- ✓ The Town Hall dates from the 17th century. Behind it on the right is a fine art nouveau building originally for Mumm champagne, with mosaics showing the champagne making process.

- ✓ Saint Remi Basilica, a Romanesque church some way south of the centre of town.

- ✓ The many champagne houses and the chalk caves that are used to store and age the champagne. Most of the houses have several guided tours throughout the day in a variety of languages for a small fee, which usally includes a sample at the end of the tour. It is a good idea to call ahead to ensure that you don't miss the tour you are interested in.

To Do

Notre-Dame Cathedral: This masterpiece of Gothic art is one of the major medieval achievements in Europe. Built in the 13th century, it features features that make it unique: its exceptional unity of style, its luminosity and the richness of its statuary. Destined to receive the coronation of the kings of France, it was provided with the most beautiful facade of the kingdom. The reverse side of the facade is unique in the world by sculptures that occupy niches that line its entire surface. Adorned with 2,303 sculptures, the cathedral of Reims is the only church to have angels with wings spread, including the famous Angel with a smile on the left portal of the facade.

The gallery of kings alone counts 56 statues of a size of 4.5 m. The interior seizes by its clarity and vertical slenderness. The nave and the choir rise on three levels: arcades, triforium, blind and high windows. The famous stained-glass windows date from the 13th century. This is the case of those of the great rose of the facade. The three windows of the axial chapel are the work of Marc Chagall (1974). The two towers reach a height of 81 m. The height under the vault of the building is 38 m and its total length is around 150 m.

Saint-Remi Basilica: This Roman-Gothic basilica is one of the most remarkable achievements of Romanesque art in the North of France. Length of 126 m, it impresses by its depth and the feeling of intimacy that it provides. It was built in the 11th century to house the relics of Saint Remi, the bishop who baptized Clovis in 498. His tomb occupies the center of the choir. The sober Romanesque nave and the fourteenth-century Gothic choir (end of the 12th century) constitute an impressive ensemble of lightness and harmony. The facade was rebuilt at the same time as the choir.

The palace of the Tau: The residence of the archbishops of Reims has adjoined the cathedral since the twelfth century, but it has assumed the classical aspect that it currently only after the transformations carried out at the end of the 17th century by Jules Hardouin -Mansart and Robert de Cotte. The Palais du Tau now houses the Musée de l'Oeuvre de Notre-Dame. The treasury of the cathedral and part of the original statuary of the church are exhibited there. The Tau room, where the banquet of the sacraments was held, is decorated with tapestries from the 15th century that tell the story of Fort Roy Clovis. The most remarkable pieces of the royal treasure of the cathedral are the talisman of Charlemagne (ninth century) and the chalice of Saint Remi (twelfth century). The reliquary of the Holy

Ampoule would contain the oil of heavenly origin from which the new king was anointed at the ceremony of his coronation.

The Saint-Remi Abbey Museum: Located in the 17th and 18th century buildings of the former Saint Remi Abbey, this museum holds important collections relating to the history of Reims from prehistory to the Second World War. The museum is structured around four sections: the history of the abbey, with the visit of the buildings which are organized around a cloister of 1709; The Gallo-Roman Reims, former refectories and kitchens of the abbey; Regional archeology, where collections from prehistory to the sixteenth century are exhibited; Military history, recalling the close link between Reims and the warlike past of France, from the Gaulish war to the Nazi surrender in 1945.

Visit Strategy

But as they all cost, visiting soon eats into your budget. The best thing about Reims is there is always something going on for free. I have lived here eight months and I don't think one month has passed without a festival or carnival.

The best by far is the Christmas Fair which fills the Place d'Erlon with a huge number of specialist stalls, great for pre-Christmas shopping.

If you like classic cars, this is a mecca, in eight months I've seen four classic rallies here.

For the kids in the summer, the traders set up a free, supervised area in the Place d'Erlon, it even has some English speaking guardians.

For a cheaper time, head down to the Place de la Republique early on a Saturday morning (7am -1 pm) to look around the market, fish, meat, cheese and bric a brac at reasonable prices, unless they realise you're a tourist! Don't feel like shopping, just wander about and soak up the atmosphere.

Reims has a vibrant theatre life. There is the main Theatre (Opera and Culture), La Comedie (20th century drama and film art), and further out the centre, La Cartonnerie (alternative, performance and music acts). It also has the Opera cinema which plays English language films, which one should note are marked V.O. on the board outside.

There is a free listing guide available in most bars and supermarkets called 'Sortie' which comes out on Thursday, which lists all the live gigs and cinema times.

To Buy

Reims has all the usual stores you'd expect in any major town. The Galeries Lafayette has menswear, womenswear, kidswear and a food hall downstairs, which sells English food at exorbitant prices if you feel homesick.

There is a small shopping centre, Espace d'Erlon, which has a Monoprix downstairs, not a bad bet to buy your Champagne at prices that aren't inflated as they are in some tourist shops. It also has a FNAC (the French equivilent of HMV) which sells CDs/ DVDs/ and Books, including English ones.

There are two wine cellars facing the cathedral, both of which sell a wide variety of champagnes at pretty much the same price as the maisons themselves, sometimes cheaper.

If you feel the need to buy English or American newspapers, there is a news stand opposite the

Gluepot (the English Pub) on the Place d'Erlon. The guy who runs it is extremely good fun and revels in the chance of speaking English.

To Eat

Traditional French Cuisine

Le Bouillon des Halles, 18, rue du Temple (on the pedestrian city centre, next to the town center and the historical Market les Halles du Boulingrin), +33(0)3 26 77 08 55. From Tuesday to Saturday. Panoramic restaurant with a superb wall of Champagne located inside a Unesco classified building, in the heart of Reims. Traditional French Cuisine, Unique Champagne Bar, artistic atmosphere . Menu from 19,80€.

The Place d'Erlon is the near beating heart of the city (It's not exactly a hotbed of activity!) . There are many great places to eat here from cheap burger bars (Q, a Belgian McD's) to Anglo-Irish bars, the best for food being the James Joyce, to the very expensive, but very good Brasserie Flo, on the corner near the station. If you go around the corner onto Boulevard Foch you will find some good mid-price eateries. The restaurant in the Hotel d'Univers is supposed to be very good, according to my local friends, but looks very intimidating from the outside. The Cote, nearer the square, is cheaper and is just as good for food. The real gem worth finding is the Aux Coteaux, mainly a pizzeria but with some nice mains as well.

If you are up by the Theatre there's quite a nice cheap Chinese cafe opposite, and next to the only McDonalds in the centre of town.

There is only one Indian restaurant in town, the Taj Mahal, on the Rue de Vesle. reasonable value, reasonable food, but Gandhi is hardly going to rise from his grave to eat there. If you go further down the Rue de Vesle you come to the Place d'Erlon. The Irish pub, The Kilberry, does food, I'm saying no more. Pizzerias here are a lot cheaper than the centre of town. All seem to charge a flat rate of E4.50 for a large pizza and the Mexicanne at the Calabraise could easily pass for Pizza Express' American Hot. They also do good mains as well. If you can't find it try the Dolce Vitae, opposite the Taj Mahal.

For better ethnic food look down the road at the side of the Opera cinema for a selection of good, cheaper, French and Ethnic restaurants (Chinese, Mexican and French). Matsuri, a small Japanese restaurant, is located next to the side entrance of Monoprix.

Real top end recommendations say if you've just sold your granny for cash try the Hotel National at the station end corner of the Place d'Erlon.

Another option is to buy a baguette at one of the many patisseries and sit by one of the fountains and watch the world go by. If this is your option try the Petit Fours, a small kiosk off the Place d'Erlon, past the Opera cinema and across the lights, it's bright yellow, you can't miss it!

Au Conti, 93, place Drouet d'Erlon (on the pedestrian city centre, next to the train station and the main historical heritage of Reims) +33(0)3 26 40 39 35, fax: +33(0)3 26 47 51 12). Every day but on Sunday evenings. Panoramic restaurant in the heart on the coronation town. Traditional French cuisine in the elegant style of a XIXth century mansion. Menu 3 courses + drink from 24,90€.

To Drink

Champagne of course!

Place de Stalingrad- There are two great places here, The Kilberry and Stalingrad. The Kilberry, an Irish pub, is where all the French drink. It's a lot cheaper than in the centre and, to my mind, has a better atmosphere. It also has lots of free music and good promotions. The manager, Mike, is generally friendly and the staff and locals are very friendly. Definitely one to watch the Rugby in. For the quieter drink, try the Stalingrad on the corner. It's a traditional French Tabac, has limited food at lunchtime. The owner, Patrick, is an English speaking Jazz fan and there is normally live Jazz upstairs on a Thursday night.

Place d'Erlon- The main street in town is home to some excellent establishments. Cochon A Plumes and the Gin Pamp are two of the few places that have happy hours. Gin Pamp, being the less expensive of the two, is typically more crowded; it also sometimes offers live music. The Cochon A Plumes, however, offers an excellent atmosphere. Other options include the microbrewery Les 3 Brasseurs, L'Apostrophe, The Shirlock Pub (where the servers wear kilts), the James Joyce, and The Gluepot.

Interested in staying out a little later? Try the LBee (complete with a small dance floor) or La Bodega! Both close around 3am. After that you will need to go to one of the few night clubs in town.

If you venture as far as the Porte de Mars, nip across to the Bar d'Anvers, across the Place de Republique, nothing out of the ordinary, but you may get involved in an interesting conversation, if you speak French and sit at the bar.

To Sleep

Best Western Hôtel de la Paix >>, +33(0)3 26 40 04 08

Grand Hôtel Continental >>, 93, place Drouet d'Erlon - 51100 Reims, +33(0)3 26 40 39 35, fax: +33(0)3 26 47 51 12),

Hotel Ibis Styles >> (Hotel Reims Centre Cathédrale), 21 boulevard Paul Doumer (51 100 Reims), +33 3 26 79 88 50, checkin: 3pm; checkout: 11am. The hotel Ibis Styles Reims is located downtown the City of Reims, close to the Convention Center, the train station of Reims Centre Ville and the Cathedral. Recently refurbished, the 3-star hotel offers 66 rooms, restaurant and bar.

Hotel Holiday Inn >> (Hotel Holiday Inn Centre Reims), 46 rue Buirette (51 100 Reims), +33 3 26 78 99 99, checkin: 3pm; checkout: 11am. The 4-

star hotel Holiday Inn Centre Reims is located in the heart of Reims, near the Place Drouet d'Erlon and the Cathedral. Recently refurbished, the 4-star hotel offers 82 rooms, italian restaurant Il Duomo and bar "In The R" on the 7th floor of the hotel.

Hotel Mercure >> (Hotel Mercure Reims Cathedrale), 31 boulevard Paul Doumer (51 723 Reims), +33 3 26 84 49 49, checkin: 3pm; checkout: 11am. Recently refurbished, the 4-star hotel Mercure Reims Cathédrale is located in the center of the city near the Cathedral and the Convention Center. It offers 126 rooms and junior suite, a restaurant with an outstanding view over the Canal of Reims, a bar and an indoor garage.

Reasonably priced hotels off the Place d'Erlon include Grand Hotel du Nord and Hotel Cristal.

Most of these hotels have a reasonably priced deal with the underground car park in Place d'Erlon, but remember to ask for a ticket at entrance to the car park and don't use your credit card, or you will end up paying twice.

The cheapest place to stay in the Place d'Erlon is the Hotel Victoria. It's family run by the Camus and has been since the war. Don't be put off by the gaudy placards outside, or the cramped bar/ reception, the rooms are large, clean, en-suite and all come with TV (French), an added advantage is free wi-fi in the bar/reception. The bar is also the cheapest place to drink in the Place d'Erlon. However, the reviews on most big hotel review sites aren't the most flattering.

If you're backpacking take a taxi from the station to C.I.S (pronounced CES) It's basic, communal kitchen and showers, but it's cheap and clean, but can get noisy if large groups are in. The bad news is it's non smoking and no booze is allowed in the place (officially!)

Sightseeing in Reims

What to see. Complete travel guide

This French town is known as the center of champagne production. The town has hundreds of underground tunnels, in which the sparkling wine is stored. Of course, you will be offered a rich list of wine in every restaurant of the town, the majority of which is champagne. However, apart from trips to restaurants tourists are offered to visit numerous exciting excursions.

Mars Gates are known as the oldest architectural structure of the town. The height of the gate's arch estimates 13 meters, and the width - 23 meters. As you might guess from the name, this monument was installed in honor of the Roman god Mars. The monument appeared during the reign of the Roman Empire. Not far away from the gate you can see the ruins of the temple, which is also dedicated to the god of war.

Reims Cathedral is one of the amazing religious buildings. Here took place the coronation ceremony of all French kings. The building was damaged badly by fire in 1914, so its restoration lasted over 5 years. Today the cathedral is widely known as UNESCO World Heritage Site.

Among other old buildings we should definitely mention Basilica of St. Remi, which construction started in the 11th century. It lasted for over 400 years and today is a mix of various architectural styles. Another historical monument, which is currently under protection of UNESCO, is the Palace of Tau, which building took place in 15 - 16 centuries. The suburbs of the town are also very picturesque as here you can see vineyards and take a walk in piedmont regions.

Admirers of painting should definitely visit the Reims Museum of Fine Arts, which was founded in 1794 and was originally located in the Town Hall building. Over the years, the museum's collection has grown hundreds of times. So it was transferred to the building of the old monastery in 1913 which is its current location. The main part of the exposition comprises collections of Renaissance paintings. The whole first floor accommodates works of art of the 20th century. There is also a collection of sculptures, engravings, and antique furniture. The church of Saint-Jacques is a remarkable object. It is the only church in the city that was not destroyed during the years of the revolution. The church was built in the 12th century and has been rebuilt repeatedly over hundreds of years. During the Great French Revolution, stables and barracks were stationed there. In the post-revolutionary period, reconstruction efforts started and are continuing at the present time. They succeeded in restoring a beautiful antique organ, antique stained-glass windows and various elements of decoration.

An incredibly beautiful architectural monument is the Basilica of St. Remigia. The very first church in its place was built in the 10th century. Nowadays, one can enjoy a luxurious building with columns and arches, erected in the 19th century. The basilica has been recognized as a UNESCO World Heritage Site. It keeps many unique religious values. On the territory of the basilica is the tomb of Saint Remigia.

The Vergè Palace Museum is located in a fabulous historical building. Its erection began in the 12th century. In the 16th century they added a new wing, so nowadays the complex of buildings looks rather unusual. In a certain period, a famous French photographer Krafft owned the mansion. Nowadays, the museum holds a collection of old photographs, as well as photographic equipment and personal belongings of the former owner. The halls of the museum have beautiful antique furniture of great value. Visitors can enjoy interesting collections of ancient engravings and paintings. Lovers of vintage cars should definitely visit the Automobile Museum. It is one of the largest in France. In total, the museum has about 200 cars, the earliest of which were produced in the early 20th century. All exhibits are maintained in excellent technical condition.

Cuisine and Restaurant

Cuisine of Reims for gourmets. Places for dinner best restaurants

Reims is a scenic French city well known for its upscale restaurants and charming cafes of international standard. The La Table Anna restaurant is the most in demand eating house of the city being the first choice place among hundreds of others among local residents and foreign guests. By its interior the restaurant resembles a classic French bistro. The guests will appreciate a vast choice of unique dishes and attractive pricing. The eating house specializes in local cuisine; one of the most noted features of the establishment is a wide assortment of desserts.

The Le Foch restaurant is another attractive place to eat and rest offering best treats of ethnic cuisine. The main speciality on the menu is a tuna fish with original tomato sauce. The guests can complete their meals with original strawberry dessert. Among other treats on the menu of the Le Foch restaurant guests will find seafood dishes. Genuine seafood gourmands will appreciate sea bream and squids with karbonara sauce. One of the most prestigious restaurants of Reims is the Le Parc Les Crayeres eating house. It is a perfect place for festive events organization. This restaurant is housed in a historical building of fantastic beauty.

The Le Parc Les Crayeres' hall will amaze with its elegant decoration, every element of the restaurant's interior is specially designed. The restaurant's menu is as perfect as its appearance is; this eating house has got several awards for high quality of its dishes and service. In addition to excellent dishes clients can order excellent sorts of champagne, the wine list of the Le Parc Les Crayeres restaurant includes a lot of rare drinks. Tourists tending to rest in a peace and quiet atmosphere are recommended to visit the Version Originale restaurant specializing in international cuisine. In the daytime a special budgetary menu is available for customers. The Version Originale restaurant offers a chance to enjoy an excellent atmosphere to rest and a vast choice of tasty dishes at affordable price.

Among the restaurants of Italian cuisine the La Trattoria eating house is the most in demand place to eat much appreciated by local residents. It serves customers till the late evening. The restaurant offers interesting entertainment programs for guests, in the daytime the restaurant is mostly visited by tourists. Genuine seafood admirers will appreciate the La Paix restaurant-café. The eating house offers to rest in a comfortable hall, decorated in bright sunny colors, and in fine weather the visitors can take a table on a scenic terrace. The restaurant offers a great choice of classic fish dishes, rare delicacies and inimitable exotic treats on the menu.

Tradition and Lifestyle

Colors of Reims traditions, festivals, mentality and lifestyle

Travelers opting to visit Reims will be interested in learning special features of character of local residents. Knowing the character of people will promote communication and avoid misunderstanding in various situations during the vacation. The main features of temper of local folks are politeness, tactfulness and restraint. The local residents are used to meet many foreign guests in the city, so they are rather friendly to travelers. Tourists may experience language problems as the local folks speak foreign languages rather unwillingly.

Local people often seem to be unwilling to interact and communicate with tourists or may seem even to experience negligence towards foreign guests however it is not true. It seems because of a rather serious attitude of local people towards culture which main element is language. Commonly local folks have a good command of other languages; however they try not to use them in everyday life.

Tourists are highly recommended to learn several simple phrases in French as the local residents will much appreciate it. The citizens are good interlocutors, they are always glad to keep a conversation in any aspects. City guests opting to negotiate with business associates need to learn several important rules.

First of all, it is important to fix an appointment a few days in advance, moreover being late to the appointment will be interpreted by locals as disrespect. But it is necessary to be diligent and accurate irrespectively of importance of the meeting; if you are late for a couple of minutes, it will be as well interpreted as a serious "offence". An optimum way to start a conversation is to touch upon neutral topics, proceeding to serious business later. Small gifts especially of intellectual meaning are welcome and will help to establish a contact and earn confidence of new people and business associates.

The matter is that education and self-improvement are highly valued by local residents. They are proud of their culture and history. Many of them are keen on philosophy and art. If interlocutor is intelligent and well informed as well as interested in poesy or philosophy, the gift will be much appreciated. Moreover it will be a guarantee of trust relations.

Books or art albums will be the best choice to present to locals being appropriate in any situation.

Culture and Sights

Culture of Reims. Places to visit old town, temples, theaters, museums and palaces

Many tourists identify Reims with the best sparkling wine, as one of the city streets locates old wine cellars, which are on the list of important touristic sights. Many cultural sights of Reims are of the worldwide significance. Among them tourist will discover the Notre-Dame being a unique historical monument. Its construction was started in 1211, and lasted for 100 years, almost all the French kings were crowned there.

Elegant stained-glass windows are the main decorative feature of the cathedral, a part of them was created following a project by Mark

Chagall. An interesting fact is that nobody has ever washed these windows during the cathedral existence. The fact they are still clean is one of the cathedral secrets.

Palais du Tau is another important architectural building. It is a former palace of archbishops. The construction of the palace was finished in 1690. The palace is located near the cathedral, at present time it hosts a museum, which keeps the most interesting collection of religious artifacts. The museum collection includes age-old tapestries, sculptures and other priceless items which were used in the crowning ceremony. The Saint-Remi basilica is a significant religious sight, as it keeps the Saint Remi's tomb. The basilica is executed in the Romanic style. Today it is the biggest pilgrim church in the north region of the country. The name of this patron saint of the city stands for name of one of the museums in Reims.

The main artifact of Saint Remi's museum is Saint Icon-Lamp being an important crowning attribute. Also the museum keeps a perfect collection of historical and archeological artifacts.

The city of Reims offers various landmarks and sights, which were established more than a thousand years ago. The Triumphal Arch is devoted to the Roman war-god Mars. According to one of the theories this historical monument was built in the 2nd century B.C. The suburban districts of Reims keep a lot of interesting landmarks and sights to visit and explore. The city is a perfect destination offering various types of leisure and numerous spots of historical and cultural interest to visit.

Top Attractions in Reims

One of the must-see destinations in the Champagne region, Reims combines the culture of a big city with the charm of a smaller town. There's plenty to see on a quick day trip from Paris (less than one hour away by TGV train) and enough to keep visitors entertained for a longer stay. Inspiring architecture and a rich heritage have earned Reims a place on France's list of "Villes d'Art et d'Histoire" (Cities of Art and History).

This historic town abounds with impressive monuments, elegant public squares, and stylish restaurants. Reims boasts three UNESCO World Heritage Sites and four Michelin-starred dining rooms. Most of all, Reims is renowned for its glorious Gothic cathedral, where French kings were crowned. Although Reims was damaged during the First and Second World Wars, the town has been marvelously rebuilt, and many of the newer buildings were designed in a lovely Art Deco style.

Cathédrale Notre-Dame de Reims

Designated a UNESCO World Heritage Site, the Cathedral of Notre-Dame stands proudly in the center of Reims with its soaring towers visible from a distance. Reims' cathedral enjoys a very special position in French history. Similar to Westminster Abbey in London, the Cathédrale Notre-Dame de Reims was used for the monarchy's coronation ceremonies (for more than eight centuries). Joan of Arc also attended mass here. This sacred monument lies on the site of a 5th-century church where Clovis, the first Christian king, was baptized. When that church was destroyed by a fire in 1210, the construction for the present cathedral began a year later.

This breathtaking 13th-century edifice is a master work of High Gothic architecture and one of the finest cathedrals in France. The vault of the nave is 38 meters high, supported externally by a flurry of flying buttresses whose technical performance is concealed behind a profusion of delicately sculpted angels. The richly patterned west front of the cathedral features three magnificent doorways, with a gorgeous rose window over the central doorway. Above this is the iconic Gallery of Kings, a long row of statues set in niches. The sculpture on the central doorway depicts the life of the Virgin.

One amusing feature of the facade is the "Sourire de Reims" (Smiling Angel). Upon entering the sanctuary, visitors are overwhelmed by the enormity of the space. The vast nave has an ambience of solemnity and is illuminated by many stained-glass windows. Although many of the original windows were destroyed, new stained-glass windows by Marc Chagall and the German artist Imi Knoebel have added a contemporary touch to the cathedral.

Address: Place du Cardinal Luçon, Reims

Palais du Tau (Archbishops' Palace)

Another UNESCO-listed monument, the Palais du Tau, adjoining the cathedral, is the former residence of archbishops. The ancient palace was almost entirely rebuilt in the 17th century in French Neoclassical style, however the building has several perfectly preserved medieval rooms. Visitors can see the royal apartments where kings stayed during their coronation ceremonies.

In these splendid surroundings, it's easy to imagine the grandeur of past royal events. The Salle de Tau, the banquet hall used after coronation ceremonies (held next door at the cathedral), is adorned with exquisite 15th-century Arras tapestries. Within the palace's 13th-century chapel, a treasury contains remarkable items, including the 9th-century talisman of Charlemagne and the 12th-century chalice of Saint Rémi. The palace also has a museum, which displays statues from the cathedral and tapestries depicting the story of King Clovis.

Address: 2 Place du Cardinal-Luçon, Reims

Basilique Saint-Rémi

The oldest church in Reims, the Basilique Saint-Rémi is an exceptional Early Romanesque monument and is listed as a UNESCO World Heritage Site. This awe-inspiring church was built between 1005 and 1049 (for a Benedictine abbey) on the site of an 8th-century Carolingian chapel, which drew many pilgrims.

Although the exterior is Gothic, the interior still has elements of the original Romanesque structure. The harmonious 11th-century nave is illuminated by 12th-century stained-glass windows, giving the sanctuary a warm and ethereal ambience, while the choir and surrounding chapels exemplify a serene Early Gothic style that inspires spiritual worship. The church houses the tomb of Saint Rémi (440-533), which has made this basilica a place of veneration since the 8th century.

During the Hundred Years' War, the abbey fell into decline and was later revived during the Renaissance. However, during the French Revolution, the monks were expelled, and the basilica was converted into a parish church. The First World War caused damage to the building, which took forty years to repair. Today, the Basilique Saint-Rémi is open to the public for visits and is occasionally used as a venue for music concerts.

Address: Place du Chanoine Ladame, Reims

Elegant Public Squares & Ancient Monuments

The first square most tourists will see in Reims city center is the Place du Cardinal-Luçon, where the cathedral, the Palais de Justice (Law Courts), and a bronze Joan of Arc statue are located. Also a must-see attraction, the expansive Place de la République boasts a well-manicured park space and an imposing 3rd-century Roman triumphal arch, the Porte de Mars, which served as a town gate until 1544.

South of the Place de la République is the Hôtel de Ville (Town Hall), constructed between 1627 and 1630. Another well-preserved 3rd-century Roman monument is the Cryptoportique, found at the Place du Forum. This archaeological site is used as a venue for summertime music concerts.

The most happening area of Reims is the Place Drouet d'Erlon, a pleasant tree-lined square with many bustling brasseries and restaurants. Dining at an outdoor terrace on this square is one of the most enjoyable things to do in Reims. At the southern end of the Place Drouet d'Erlon stands the second oldest church in Reims, the Eglise Saint-Jacques, which dates from the 12th to 16th centuries. The most elegant square in Reims is the Place Royale lined with handsome Neoclassical buildings and featuring a bronze statue of King Louis XV at the center.

Musée des Beaux Arts

As would be expected from a "City of Art and History," Reims has an excellent fine arts museum. The permanent collection includes an extensive array of paintings, drawings, statues, art objects, and antique furniture. The collection covers French and European artworks from the

16th to the 20th centuries, showing the evolution of art from the Renaissance to the modern era. Highlights include the religious art; 19th-century landscape paintings; and Impressionist paintings by masters such as Monet, Renoir, and Pissarro.

Address: 8 Rue Chanzy, Reims

Musée Saint-Rémi

This wonderful history museum is housed in various rooms of the former royal abbey of Saint-Rémi, an architectural jewel that is listed as a UNESCO World Heritage Site. The buildings reveal centuries-old architectural aspects, such as the cloister, a grand staircase, and the chapter house a masterpiece of Romanesque art featuring intricately carved 12th-century capitals. The museum collection includes art objectsand antiquities, such as archaeological finds from the

Gallo-Roman era. This museum is one of the best places to visit to learn about the history of Reims, from ancient times through the Renaissance period.

Address: 53 Rue Simon, Reims

Musée Hôtel Le Vergeur

On the Place du Forum, the Musée Hôtel le Vergeur displays a unique collection in a fabulous 13th-century mansion. The Hôtel Le Vergeur takes its name from the wealthy Vergeur family who owned the house until the 16th century. The previous owner, Hugues Krafft, devoted much of his fortune to restoring the house. He decorated the rooms with splendid furniture and created an art collection consisting of objects brought back from his many trips abroad.

Today, the museum displays Krafft's decorative arts collection, as well as an eclectic assortment of prints and paintings that illustrate the history of Reims; objects that were part of royal coronations; and exceptional pieces of religious art, most notably the engravings by Albrecht Dürer.

Address: 36 Place du Forum, Reims

Chapelle Foujita

The Japanese artist of the Ecole de Paris, Tsuguharu Foujita was so inspired by a visit to the Basilique Saint-Rémi that he decided to convert to Christianity. His baptism took place on October 14, 1959 at the Cathédrale Notre-Dame de Reims, and he received the baptismal name, Leonard.

In 1965, with the financial support of René Lalou and with a single-minded artistic vision, Leonard Foujita built his very own chapel in Reims. The Chapelle Foujita was designed entirely by Foujita, from start to finish. He oversaw the architectural plans and supervised the construction of the building. Foujita then designed the sketches for the ironwork and stained-glass windows, and next he painted the frescoes in the chapel's choir.

Foujita chose the Romanesque style for the chapel because it recalls the Saint-Rémi Basilica and because a simplistic Romanesque structure would be ideal for displaying his exquisitely detailed murals. Foujita's sense of spirituality and artistic panache shines through in each scene of his monumental work adorning the chapel.

Address: 33 Rue du Champ de Mars, Reims

Musée de la Reddition (World War II Museum)

In a listed historic building, this museum is dedicated to the remembrance of the Second

World War. The museum is housed in the building where Eisenhower's headquarters and the Operations Room of the Allied Forces were located during WWII. Most importantly, this building is where the German General Jodl announced unconditional surrender on May 7, 1945, ending the war. The news was then announced simultaneously in the Allied capitals on May 8, 1945.

The building has been preserved in its original condition and gives visitors a vivid impression of the historical events. The exhibits show the role of Reims at the end of a full-scale war. From Occupation to Liberation, the story of the war is told through objects, documents, memorabilia, and models. There is also interesting information about the French Resistance.

Address: 12 Rue du Franklin Roosevelt, Reims

Festivals

Every year in spring or early summer (dates vary), Reims transforms itself into the scene of a medieval celebration for Les Fêtes Johanniques, the Joan of Arc Festival. The festival reenacts the Saint's arrival in Reims, after her military victories, for the coronation of King Charles VII. The city commemorates this historical event (which took place on July 17, 1429) with authentic pageants, an artisan crafts market, musical performances, and other street entertainment.

During the festival's Grand Coronation parade, town residents dress up in period costumes to follow "Joan of Arc" and "King Charles VII" in a procession to the Notre-Dame Cathedral.

Another lively cultural event is Les Sacres du Folklore, which brings together folk singers, musicians, and dancers from across the globe. The festival takes place for several days in June or July and features dance performances, music concerts, and a gala event.

Where to Stay in Reims: Best Areas & Hotels

The city of Reims offers a wide variety of accommodations from upscale luxury hotels to affordable budget lodging. The most upscale properties are surrounded by tranquil parklands, appealing to those who prefer a more resort-like ambience in an idyllic rural setting.

Luxury Hotels: Surrounded by a lush seven-hectare parkland, the (Domaine Les Crayères) is a sumptuous five-star Relais & Châteaux property. Lodging is in a lovely château or a charming cottage; both have generously sized rooms adorned in classical French style. The hotel's outstanding guest services include a concierge, airport transfers, valet parking, self parking, and dry cleaning. Guests may also borrow bicycles during their stay.

The hotel boasts two superb restaurants: Restaurant Le Parc, with two Michelin stars, and the modern, casual Brasserie le Jardin. A gourmet continental breakfast is served every morning in a beautiful dining room. The Domaine Les Crayères is in the outskirts of Reims, within walking distance of the Basilique Saint-Rémi.

Another Relais & Châteaux property, the five-star (L'Assiette Champenoise) blends luxurious comfort with modern style. Guest rooms are stylishly minimalistic, with park or garden views. Gourmet food lovers should note that the hotel's restaurant has three Michelin stars, the highest rating. The restaurant serves the finest local seasonal cuisine in an attractive dining room or on the outdoor terrace. Breakfast is available in the dining room or delivered to guests' rooms.

For added convenience, the hotel offers room service, free valet parking, and assistance in booking tours. Guests may also take advantage of the property's gardens and stunning indoor pool. L'Assiette Champenoise is located in the town of Tinqueux, three kilometers (a 10-minute drive) from Reims.

The (Best Western Premier Hotel de la Paix) is well situated in the heart of Reims, just a short walk away from the Cathédrale Notre-Dame de Reims and the Musée des Beaux-Arts. This four-star hotel offers luxurious, contemporary-style rooms and conveniences such as on-site parking and 24-hour concierge service. Guests will also appreciate the indoor swimming pool, restaurant, spa, sauna, and hammam. A continental breakfast buffet is available for an additional charge.

Mid-Range Hotels: In the historic heart of the city, the four-star (Holiday Inn Reims Centre) is within walking distance of the cathedral and other top tourist attractions. This recently refurbished modern hotel has simple but stylish guest rooms, and conveniences such as room service and parking. Other amenities include a front desk open 24 hours with multilingual staff, laundry services, a business center, and babysitting. A breakfast buffet is available for an additional charge.

For convenience and comfort, the (Mercure Reims Centre Cathédrale) is a great choice near the historic center, about a 10-minute walk from the cathedral. This four-star hotel has a 24-hour front desk, business center, and parking. The soundproofed guest rooms feature a sleek contemporary style, updated bathrooms, wide-screen televisions, and refrigerators. Specializing in authentic French cuisine, the hotel's restaurant serves breakfast, lunch, and dinner. Room service is also available.

The (Golden Tulip Reims L Univers) is located near the train station about a 10-minute walk from the cathedral and other landmarks in the historic center of town. This convenient four-star hotel has a 24-hour front desk with multilingual staff, concierge services, and a restaurant serving lunch and dinner. The soundproofed rooms feature modern decor and premium bedding. A breakfast buffet and room service are available.

Budget Hotels: In the historic center of Reims near the bustling Place Drouet d'Erlon, the (Hôtel des Arcades) is within easy walking distance of the cathedral and the museum of fine arts. The hotel offers basic rooms at an affordable price, but has considerable style and sleek modern bathrooms for a two-star property. A continental breakfast buffet is available.

The (Hôtel Ibis Reims Centre) is conveniently located near the historic city center within walking distance of many top tourist attractions. This three-star hotel offers excellent value without compromising on style. The hotel has a 24-hour front desk (with multilingual staff) and snack bar, as well as laundry services. A breakfast buffet is available for an additional charge.

For those on a tight budet who don't mind very basic accommodations, the (Résidence Hôtelière Laudine) is a good option on the outskirts of town near the Basilique Saint-Rémi. The small, simple guest rooms include kitchenettes with refrigerators and microwaves. A self-service laundry facility and parking are also available. Guests may choose to pay an additional fee for a breakfast buffet in the cafeteria.

Palace of Tau

The Episcopal Palace next-door is where the cathedral's treasury is kept, and also had a role in the coronation ritual.

The king would come here to don his robes, and from 990 to 1825 this was where the post-coronation banquet would happen. On display is an astonishing assortment of tapestries, reliquaries and statues.

Among the must-sees is a 9th-century talisman belonging to Charlemagne. But nothing can match the Holy Ampulla for importance: It contained the anointing oil for every coronation from Louis VII in 1131 to Louis XVI in 1774.

Villa Demoiselle

Next to the Pommery Caves is a gorgeous mansion built during the transition between art nouveau and art deco at the start of the 20th century.

After being left to rot in the 80s and 90s it was done up in 2004: The president of Vranken Champagnes, Paul-François Vranken spared no expense restoring the villa to its Belle Époque splendour.

Some sublime pieces of furniture and decoration were also added, like sinuous chairs crafted by Gustave Serrurier-Bovy, and a Cuir de Cordoue ceiling Émile Gallé.

There's also a fireplace by a student of Louis Majorelle, which was submitted to the Exposition Universelle in Paris in 1900.

Saint-Remi Basilica

This church is a UNESCO World Heritage Site and acclaimed as a gothic masterpiece for its sculptural decoration and architecture.

Parts of the building are much older than the gothic period, as the romanesque nave and transepts are from the 1000s.

Later gothic additions like the choir ambulatory and facade are masterful in the way they help form a unified whole.

The historic relics of Reims' patron saint are inside: Saint-Remi was the bishop noted for baptising Clovis the King of Franks around the turn of the 6th century

The Ruins at the Hotel le Vergeur

Bits of architecture from a town destroyed in World War I now decorate this hotel garden.

In the ancient French city of Reims there is a magnificent turreted townhouse that dates from the 13th century, holding a remarkable secret: a rarely visited garden filled with architectural ruins. Collected by one man following the armistice of 1918, this haunting graveyard of forgotten doorways, columns, and archways tells the story of one France's most historic cities, and its almost complete destruction during World War I.

Located in the bucolic Champagne-Ardennes region of northeastern France, Reims has been the traditional crowning site of the kings of France since the 11th century. The old city is dominated by the 800-year-old cathedral of Notre-Dame de Reims, while the countryside is dotted with the vineyards of prestigious champagne houses, like Veuve Clicquot, that go back hundreds of years.

But the historic beauty and charm of this bucolic city was all but wiped from the face of the Earth during World War I. As the German army poured through Belgium and into France in the autumn of 1914, Reims became a key strategic target both tactically, as it was a gateway to Paris, about 80 miles away, and in terms of French morale. The city was swiftly captured just a month after war had been declared, although the Germans only occupied the city for eight days, until the Allied victory at the Marne forced them to withdraw.

Unable to recapture Reims, the Germans decided to reduce it to ruins. For four years, the German artillery pulverized the ancient city, all but obliterating it. High explosives and incendiary shells rained upon the city almost continually, as fire engulfed the city. On April 1st, 1917 alone, over 2,800 shells exploded on Reims. The next night, a further 2,100 shells fell on the city. By 1918 most of Reims had simply disappeared into ruins. But remnants of the city's architectural heritage lay dotted around the devastation and would have been lost forever if not for the efforts of one man.

Hugues Krafft was born in Paris to a German father in 1853, but moved to Reims in the late 19th century to work in the lucrative champagne trade. Looking to buy a suitably grand home, he purchased an old town house, called the Hotel le Vergeur, which overlooked the old market square, where linens, wheat, and champagne had been traded for centuries.

The turreted home was severely damaged in WWI. In the 1920s, Krafft restored most of the townhouse to its original beauty, but left one wrecked section standing. That is the Pavilion

Coquebert. The crumbling masonry and blasted architecture of the Pavilion, which dates to the 17th century, gives a poignant glimpse into how the rest of the devastated city would have looked in 1918.

As the ruins of Reims were torn down to make way for new construction, Krafft searched through the rubble for the remnants of the city's historic past. He saved doorways, lintels, whole facades, columns, archways and tombs and brought them to the garden of the Hotel le Vergeur, where he created his garden of ruins. For the interior of the hotel, he salvaged fireplaces, libraries, and artwork.

He collected part of a wall from the 17th century Hotel Lagoilie de Courtagnon, from whose wrought iron balcony Marie Antoinette watched her husband Louix XVI leave the cathedral to go to the Abbey Saint-Remi to touch sufferers from tuberculosis. Elsewhere in the garden can be found an entire facade from a majestic town house, an entrance to a 6th century Benedictine monastery, a 16th century tomb of a Knight of Malta, one of the legendary Knights Hospitaller of the Order of Saint John.

Following his death in 1935, he left the collection to the Societe des Amis du Vieux Reims, where it still rests today.

Walking through the beautiful, and often deserted gardens of the Hotel le Vergeur is a similar experience to visiting an empty historic cemetery. Covered in ivy and still bearing the scars of endless shrapnel and artillery fire, the carefully collected architectural ruins speak to the four years of horror as the German shelling gradually destroyed the ancient city.

Today, Reims, with its historic cathedral surrounded by luxurious champagne houses and vineyards, is once again a bustling tourist destination. Walking through the city it is hard to imagine that nearly everything you see is not even a century old. That is, unless you venture into the walled garden of the Hotel le Vergeur, and stroll through the scattered ruins of the lost city.

The School Where Germany Surrendered

This small red school was where Germany signed their surrender during WWII.

Ralph Morse was a war photographer working for Life magazine covering the American advance through Western Europe. One night in early May 1945, he was working in a Parisian hotel room, writing captions for some of his photographs, when there was an urgent knock at his door. A U.S. Army press officer burst in saying, as he told

Time Magazine years later, "grab your cameras, let's go."

Outside waited a staff Cadillac and four jeeps. Remembering the night nearly 70 years later for Time, Morse recalled, "I'd be damned if I was going to let my cameras get soaked, so I jumped into the Caddy. We started off, and right away we all knew we were headed for Reims. You could feel it."

Reims is an ancient city steeped in history. Located around 90 miles north east of Paris, its cathedral had been the traditional crowning site for the old Kings of France for nearly a thousand years. Morse and the speeding press convoy weren't heading for the majestic Notre Dame cathedral however, but an anonymous school house across the street from the train station on the outskirts of the city. Despite its smaller stature, the small red roofed school would nonetheless bear witness to an event of even more historic importance.

"We got to the little red schoolhouse," the photographer remembered, "and learned that the Germans were coming to sign the surrender documents in about ten minutes."

Today, the still functioning school is called the Lycee Roosevelt; back in 1945, it was known as le College Moderne et Technique de Reims. It was also happened to be the commandeered home of the operational headquarters of SHAEF, the Supreme Headquarters of the Allied Expeditionary Force, headed by General Dwight D. Eisenhower.

In the early hours of the morning of May 7th, the German delegation entered the school, led by Generaloberst Alfred Jodl, commander of the

Wehrmacht, and designated representative of Admiral Karl Donitz. According to Adolf Hitler's last will and testament, Donitz had been appointed his successor following Hitler's suicide on April 30th in Berlin. At 2:41am, Jodl signed the document on behalf of the German High Command, effectively signaling his country's unconditional surrender and ending the war in Europe.

The document was also signed by General Bedell Smith for the Allies, General Ivan Susloparov for the USSR, and witnessed by General Francois Sevez of France. But as German forces through Western Europe laid down their arms, brutal fighting continued along the Eastern Front. The Soviet high command refused to acknowledge the surrender at Reims, maintaining that the official surrender should be signed in Berlin. General Ferdinand Schorner commanding the

German army in the East, addressed his troops, "the struggle in the west however is over. But there can be no question of surrender to the Bolsheviks."

Threatening the further destruction of Berlin, Eisenhower swiftly ordered the the commanders-in-chief of the German army, air force, and navy to the capital where another surrender was signed on May 8th, placating the Soviets. The day was marked in history as VE Day.

Today the small, otherwise anonymous school is still open, but renamed in honor of President Franklin D. Roosevelt. The left hand side of the building features a small museum where the historic signing took place, whilst outside of the building is marked by the flags of the United States, Great Britain, Russia, and France. Written onto the wall are the words, "C'est ici que le 7 mai 1945, a ete signe l'acte qui mit fin a la deuxieme guerre mondiale en Europe." which translates to, "It is here that on 7 May 1945, was signed the act that ended the Second World War in Europe."

Joan of Arc Statue

An image of the legendary saint stands in the shadow of a cathedral she liberated.

This Third Republic-era statue (created in the late 19th century) portrays the legendary Joan of Arc, a warrior, mystic, martyr, and saint who saved the city of Reims from destruction at the hands of the English army. It stands in the shadow of the very cathedral she helped protect.

Born into a peasant family, the young Joan had witnessed English forces burn her village to the ground, making her family refugees. This understandably fueled her anger toward the occupying invaders. As such, her determination to fight the English made her a key figure in the battles of the Hundred Years' War, particularly the March to Reims. Her liberation of the Reims Cathedral allowed Charles VII of France to be crowned king.

Paul Dubois's image of her in Reims, crafted from bronze, portrays the "Maid of Orleans" as a wide-eyed woman with a noticeably ethereal demeanor as she gazes at the spires of the cathedral. Her facial expression perhaps hints at the mysticism at the heart of her life. But what this statue really shows is a depiction of a ferocious woman who is at ease in a world of warfare.

One of Joan of Arc's steel-clad arms is held aloft, raising an épée bâtarde longsword, while her other hand grips the reigns of her war-horse. The beast itself is powerfully built, its nostrils flaring and its hoof pawing the ground in readiness to charge.

Needless to say, this is definitely not a figure you would want to see on a dark night, and certainly not if you were an English-allied Burgundian soldier in Reims during 1429, when Joan of Arc and her 12,000-strong army besieged the city. Indeed, in such a scenario, a mere glimpse of her closeup likely would have been the last sight you ever saw before being cut down by a strike of her longsword.

Know Before You Go
You can walk by the statue at any time.

Faux de Verzy

Hundreds of dwarf beeches create an unusual, haunting forest in the north of France.

Dwarf beech trees top out at 4 or 5 meters (or roughly 15 feet) and are notable for the wide spread of their boughs and the dramatic forms they assume. They can be found in Germany, Sweden, and Denmark, as well as multiple locations in France. However, the Faux de Verzy national forest contains nearly 1000 of the hauntingly beautiful trees, making it the largest concentration of dwarf beeches in the world.

The forest's name comes from the word fau(plural: faux), which was the beech tree's name in Old French, derived from the Latin fagus (the modern French word for beech, hêtre, comes from German). The earliest mention of the existence of dwarf beeches in the area is found in a book from the nearby St-Basle Abbey and dates all the way back to the 6th century. It is unclear what led to their proliferation but speculation abounds, including suggestions that they abbey monks had a hand in spreading the relatively rare trees locally as well as abroad.

The peculiar characteristics of the dwarf beeches—which include not only their striking appearance but also their longevity (with specimens found up to 350 years old) and their abilities to fuse branches and propagate from aerial limbs—have been conclusively proven to be the result of genetic mutation, but the origin of this genetic mutation remains unknown. One popular guess chalked it up to a local pathogen; this seemed possible given the existence (in much smaller numbers) of dwarf oaks and chestnuts in the area as well, but analysis undertaken to test this theory failed to yield any evidence.

The Faux de Verzy features a marked footpath through a fenced reserve so that visitors can view these curious trees without doing damage to their delicate root structures. Some of the more spectacular specimens have been given nicknames, such as the Umbrella Fau, the Ox-Head Fau, and the Fau of the Bride. The Maiden's Fau is so-named because legend has it that Joan of Arc once napped at the foot of the tree. Strangely, dwarf beeches are surprisingly intertwined with the story of Joan of Arc, as the town of her birth boasted a famous dwarf beech that was mentioned eleven separate times at her trial.

Know Before You Go
There's no optimal season to visit the Faux, beautiful 365 out of 365 days a year. Really easy walk. Access to most areas possible with wheelchairs and strollers. Dogs are welcome. Car park well indicated.

Oise Aisne American Cemetery, Plot E

This secret cemetery where no flag is allowed to fly holds the bodies of American soldiers convicted of heinous crimes during WWII.

Plots A-D of the Oise Aisne American Cemetary hold the remains of American soldiers who died fighting in a small portion of Northern France during World War I. However set across the street unmarked and completely surrounded by impassible shrubbery is Plot E, a semi-secret fifth plot that contains the nearly forgotten bodies of a number of American soldiers who were executed for crimes committed during and after World War II.

Over 6,000 soldiers are buried in the first four plots of the Oise Aisne Cemetery, but just 94 bodies are currently buried in the shunned fifth plot. While the small patch of land is technically on the grounds of the greater cemetery, it is not easily distinguished as it sits across the street, hidden behind the tall hedges that surround it. The only way into the secret cemetery is through the superintendent's office.

The soldiers eventually interred in Plot E were tried for rape, murder, and in one case, desertion (although the remains of the deserter, Eddie Slovik, the only American executed for desertion in WWII, were returned to the states in 1987). After being convicted in U.S. courts martial held in Europe, the men were dishonorably discharged and executed via hanging or firing squad. In many cases, the men who were buried in Plot E were initially buried close to the site of their execution. Those bodies were later exhumed and moved to Oise Aisne in 1949 when the plot of shame was established.

Plot E has been referred to as an anti-memorial. No US flag is permitted to fly over the plot and the graves themselves, small in-ground stones the size of index cards, have no names; they are only differentiated by numbers. Even underground they are set apart with each body buried in Plot E positioned with its back to the main cemetery. The site does not exist on maps of the cemetery, and is not mentioned on their site.

Know Before You Go
Plot E is hidden from view by hedges. It is accessible only through a locked door in the back of the cemetery superintendent's office.

Best Brunch and Breakfast Spots in Reims

Breakfasts and brunches can make or break a day. In Reims, many cafes, bakery and restaurant owners know this and so offer splendid breakfast and brunch options. Discover the most delightful at the following locations.

Pain & Cie
Deli, Restaurant, French, Fast Food
+33326037757

Pain & Cie is a cozy French deli which offers a most popular brunch on Sundays. Copious and tasty, this brunch offers both sweet and savory delights, from yogurts with cereals, hams, cheeses, salmon, eggs, breads, jams as well as refreshing or warming drinks. Focusing on offering top quality items, Pain & Cie uses organic and artisan ingredients where it can. Pain & Cie provides seating both inside the restaurant and out on the terrace, the latter being perfect for warm summer mornings.

En Appart' Thé

A tea connoisseur's heaven, En Appart' Thé is a classic brunch spot in Reims. This tea salon, just a short walk away from the Museé des Beaux-Arts, is the perfect place to relax and enjoy their excellent beverages alongside pastries, which can either be consumed on site or as a take out. En Appart' Thé offers an outstanding Sunday brunch, French style, offering a range of fresh breads and cheeses, as well as meats, grapes and drinks included in the price. Wonderful flavors alongside a welcoming and friendly environment, make En Appart' Thé a brunch spot not to be missed.

En Appart' Thé, 23 Rue Chanzy, Reims, France, +33 3 26 02 58 94

Chez Lou
Reims, Grand Est, , 51100, France
Chez Lou prides itself for its creativity, bringing the people of Reims healthy, high-quality and

environmentally friendly food. The environment has special place in Chez Lou's heart, so at this venue, the ingredients are seasonally produced and locally sourced as well as being up to 70% biological. Enjoy a varied menu, particularly promising for bagel-lovers, as here you can choose from a list of eight different fillings and three bread types. Aside from artisan bagels, there are also soups, dessert items, salads and a vast selection of drinks. Chez Lou also caters for gluten intolerants and vegans.

Pâtisserie Manon
Pâtisserie Manon, 11 Cours Jean Baptiste Langlet, Reims, France, +33 03 26 08 07 38
Located a few steps away from the Notre Dame Cathedral in Reims is Pâtisserie Manon, a establishment with a tea salon, a tarterie, and a pâtisserie included. Sample the fresh breads, home-baked cakes and pastries made and sold at this wonderful location, which offers fantastic

sweet and savory breakfast and brunch options. It's light with happy pink tones so visiting Pâtisserie Manon is enough to make anyone's day cheerful, especially after a satisfying late morning meal.

Patisserie la Bonbonnière
Bakery, Patisserie, Tea Room, French, Tea , Pastries
+33326476552
The Patisserie la Bonbonnière is a classic French bakery, offering heavenly delights, such as pastries, fresh breads as well as fresh salads and warming beverages. Having opened its doors more than 50 years previously, this bakery, with a tea salon attached, serves breakfast, lunch or items perfect for an evening break. Make the most of a late breakfast at the Patisserie la Bonbonnière, for an experience that you will want to repeat over and over again.

Le Four à Bois

Bakery, French, Fast Food, Pastries, $$$
100 , Rue Chanzy, , Reims, Grand Est, , 51100, France
+33326474436

Offering a traditional French breakfast menu, Le Four à Bois is a breakfast spot not to miss. As the name of the bakery suggests, the breads are all baked in a wood-oven using traditional baker's methods and bio-flour to bring out the best flavor of each loaf. Situated in the heart of Reims, Le Four à Bois is the perfect spot to enjoy the aromas and flavors of an authentic French breakfast, including hot and cold drinks and delicious pastries.

Waïda et Fils
5 , Place Drouet d'Erlon, , Reims, Grand Est, , 51100, France
+33326474449

Waïda et Fils is another excellent bakery offering a cozy tea salon where the breakfast experience is simply heavenly, or make the most of the outside terrace and enjoy some people-watching. Start your day at Waïda el Fils, where you can taste the best of croissants, *pains au chocolat*, fruit tarts, pretty cakes and macaroons alongside some warming and aromatic beverages. Don't miss out on this popular bakery for a delightful and relaxed breakfast.

Best Coffee Shops in Reims

Reims, a city in the north-east of France, is famous for its champagne and for being the Coronation capital' of France pre-revolution of course. The city also plays host to great cafes here are the best Reims has to offer.

Café du Palais
14, place Myron Herrick, 51100 Reims, France, +33 3 26 47 52 54
Since its opening in 1930 – making it one of the oldest cafes in Reims – until the present day, the Café du Palais has been entertaining patrons in

its historic city center establishment. The family-run bistro has a wide selection of hot and cold drinks, snacks, meals and delicious desserts. These can all be enjoyed under the spectacular art-deco, stained-glass ceiling. While you're there, be sure to admire the eclectic photos, paintings and various figurines that adorn the interior. It is as much a curiosity shop as it is a cafe.

Le Café de Reims
85 , Place Drouet d'Erlon, , Reims, Grand Est, , 51100, France
+33326401632
Great quality service is on the menu in this typical French brasserie. You'll find a selection of hot drinks – the *café gourmand* is particularly tasty. There are also cold beverages, both alcoholic and non-alcoholic. This includes, somewhat unsurprisingly, a wide selection of wines. There's also a number of main meals and

desserts to choose from at very reasonable prices. Choose to have your coffee indoors. Alternatively, sit out on the terrace where, since Le Café de Reims is situated on one of Reims most popular streets, you can watch the world go by.

Pain et Compagnie
68 Place Drouet d'Erlon, Reims, 51100, France
+33326037757
Pain et Compagnie is half bakery, half cafe, but a 100 percent enjoyable dining experience. The cafe, which is located on the ever-popular Place Drouet d'Erlon in the very center of Reims, is open throughout the day. It serves great quality coffees, cold drinks and freshly baked pastries to tourists and locals. If you're there in summer be sure to try one of their ice-cream desserts. These are just as pleasing on the eye as they are on the tastebuds.

Harold

27 , Passage du Commerce, , Reims, Grand Est,
, 51100, France
+33326076696

The menu of this Reims' coffee shop changes from week to week but everything is always made fresh on site. On entering the charmingly decorated cafe you'll be greeted by the glass-fronted cake counter, filled to the brim with freshly baked goods for you to sample. The *formule Goûter*(the sample menu), which includes a dessert and a hot or cold drink, is an inexpensive way to try the best of what Harold has to offer. Unsurprisingly, Harold is a popular Reims hotspot, so booking is advised if you want to avoid disappointment.

Columbus Café & Co.

6 , Rue de Vesle, , Reims, Grand Est, , 51100, France
+33967443869

Columbus Café & Co. is very much a coffee shop *à la française.* Here you'll find a Gallic take on the traditional American coffee house chains. The Reims branch of this France-wide coffee house takes pride in its freshly roasted coffees. You can have your coffee to stay in or take out, a choice which is something of a rarity in French coffee shops. Also impressive is its vast array of cold drinks, including fresh-fruit smoothies, iced teas, milkshakes and coffee frappes.

Le Lion de Belfort
37, Place Drouet d'Erlon, 51100 Reims, France, +33 3 26 47 48 17
The Lion de Belfort in the very heart of Reims should be on everybody's to-do list when in this northern French city. With opening hours from early in the morning until, well, early the next morning, there's really no excuse not to visit. Le Lion de Belfort has many faces, serving everything from breakfast and brunch to lunch

and dinner. Its prime location means that it's a great place to enjoy a cup of coffee at any time of the day.

Waïda et Fils
5 , Place Drouet d'Erlon, , Reims, Grand Est, , 51100, France
+33326474449
When you hear the phrase 'French pastries' the image that conjures up in your mind probably isn't too far away from the reality of Waïda et Fils' shop window. Under its candy-striped awning, an enticing display of the finest pastries, *viennoiseries* and brightly colored macarons invite you into this bakery-cum-cafe. It is located in Reims' bustling central square. Aside from delicious sweet treats, there's also a small but carefully chosen menu. And, of course, there are the all-important great quality coffees which you can enjoy in the art-deco inspired interior.

Chez Lou

Reims, Grand Est, , 51100, France
This self-proclaimed 'creative food' cafe is one-of-a-kind in Reims. As well as the usual Americanos, cappuccinos, lattes and frappes, Chez Lou offers customers a wide selection of less traditional beverages. There is everything from seasonal fruit teas and luxury Japanese Sencha teas to fresh-fruit smoothies and the house detox health-drink. The fresh, wholesome snacks on offer make great accompaniments. Chez Lou is also committed to promoting healthy eating, using only fresh, seasonal produce and respecting the environment. So, you can leave with a happy conscience as well as a satisfied appetite.

The End

Printed in Great Britain
by Amazon